# Ear Candling for Healing

# Terms and Conditions

# Table of Contents

# Foreword

Ear Candling is a process that goes back as far as biblical times, when hollow reeds from swamp regions were used as candles. It has been passed down for numerous generations by the North and South American natives, in addition to the Egyptian, African, Oriental and European cultures.

The procedure had been essentially lost for many years, but has come back into practice once again and is now being utilized by a wide assortment of individuals.

# Chapter 1:



# Synopsis

Ear candling, likewise called ear coning or thermal-auricular therapy, and is an alternative medicine procedure claimed to better general health and well-being by lighting one end of a hollow candle and putting the other end in the ear canal.

# Background

According to some medical researchers, it's both dangerous and ineffective. Claims that the practice moves out earwax are not supported by any evidence according to some studies. The claim by one manufacturer that ear candles initiated with the Hopi tribe has likewise been disproven.

However many say the candles are a gentle and natural alternative to ear syringing. They say that the heat energy from the candle relieves pain and discomfort in the ear.

The ingredients infused in the cotton vaporize and are drawn down the hollow centre of the candle thru a 'chimney effect'. Impurities are pulled out of the ear, into the candle and either burned away or accumulated in the filter.

Both ears have to be treated, and the treatment takes around a half an hour. A calming facial massage is commonly performed afterwards, draining the sinuses, reinforcing lymph action and blood flow.

As well people claim that Ear Candling is likewise a good treatment to have if recovering from a cold or 'flu, or simply to de-stress and clear the head. The aromatherapy effects of the candle encourage relaxation and stress reduction.

# Chapter 2:

## *How Is Ear Candling Supposed To Work*

# Synopsis

It is said that if the body is under tension the flow of energy decreases till it is let go of or entirely blocked. You might not be aware of this at the start, but one of these days symptoms will appear in the body.

# The Theory

If this energy gets blocked in the head area, or once excessive ear wax develops, you might develop conditions such as stuffed up sinuses or sinusitis, headaches, earaches, dizziness or vertigo, small hearing loss, raw throat or coughing, allergies or upper respiratory tract infections. If they're not cleared up, the flow of energy slows up and pain or discomfort commonly sets in.

The removal of ear wax is a really small part of ear candling, as a matter of fact, seldom is any ear wax pulled out at all. Ear wax is necessary to our well-being.

It acts as a shock absorber for sound waves, and along with the hairs in our ears, it barricades dust particles and foreign material that may pierce the ear drum. It's when we have wax build up induced by noise, pollution, dust, and so forth, nevertheless that issues may arise.

The burning candle behaves like a chimney and draws from the ear. The drawing effect, in addition to the warmth of the candle are said to relax the body, therefore giving back to the body the power to heal itself.

Once relaxed, the body begins to function by nature to heal itself; the wax begins to move again, the circulation comes back to the whole head area.

In the external ear, we have reflex or pressure points, (the same as in hand and foot reflexology). As we work around the ear space, these reflex points are energized by the warmth of the candle and the stimulation of these reflexes may assist in wellness of additional areas of the body as well.

Ear Candling is likewise a Spiritual Therapy. When the candle is burning, we might feel free to visualize issues, fears or guilt being devoured by the flame. Once they're gone, we are free to move on. Ear Candling consequently may be effective by cleaning the inner self or emotions likewise.

# Chapter 3:



---

# Synopsis

If you're suffering with sinus issues or even hay fever, many people wholeheartedly recommend putting aside any reservations you might have about ear candling and giving it a go. But let's have a closer look at the issue.

# A Look At The Connection

If you're suffering from a bad sinusitis, then you're more susceptible to sinus ear issues. If your sinuses get congested (sinusitis nose congestion), infected or inflamed, it's much simpler for your ears to experience the same foul condition.

Most individuals might not be aware of the connection between the sinuses in the cheekbones, the nasal areas and the ears through the auditory tube. This connects the sinuses into the internal ear and this connection makes it simpler for the infections to spread from the sinuses to the ear.

The Eustachian tube's slender bent shape is really inviting to infections. If water accidentally gets into the ear, this tube gathers up the water which can't be drained and consequently invites bacterial growth which will then induce an ear infection.

A sinus infection on the other hand is most generally known as hay fever or cold, but commonly, it's an infection in the sinus cavities. This sort of infection commonly begins from congestion and a little stuffiness in the sinus cavities.

The stuffiness will then induce excessive production of mucus thinking that there are bacteria or dirt and attempts to do away with it. When inordinate mucus is produced and there's a presence of a foreign invader like bacteria, this will then induce irritation and inflammation in the sinus cavity. Due to the swelling up of the sinuses, the mucus can't properly drain and will then grow into an infection causing sinusitis and sinus ear issues.

Due to the association between the ears and the sinuses, any congestion that might happen in the sinuses may then move into the ears simply by sneezing.

When you sneeze, the air from your sinus cavities will attempt to escape through different portals inside its range, including the ears. When sneezing happens, the air is pressed through the Eustachian tube and this air may push the bacteria, along with the infection, into the auditory canal and this might cause sinus ear issues.

How may you get rid and prevent sinus ear issues? Some suggest candling but some say simply by cleansing the sinus cavities each morning and evening utilizing saline solution, you are able to get rid of the congestion and bring down the swelling to allow your sinuses to work expeditiously.

This may supply you relief from sinusitis and sinus ear issues. If you unceasingly maintain the cleanliness of your ear canals, this may keep you away from sinus ear issues. You might use cotton-tipped cleaners to take away excessive dirt and wax to prevent the ear from becoming attractive to bacteria.

A different way for you to prevent sinus ear issues is to keep your hands clean. Remember that sustaining the cleanliness of your hands may keep you free from infection and healthy.

If you're going through frequent sinus infections due to allergies, make certain to always keep your antihistamines handy to forestall excessive mucus production.

On the other hand, if you're suffering from sinus ear issues or any type of ear infections frequently, then you ought to consult an ENT specialist for further medications that may help you solve your ear issues.

# Chapter 4:

## *About Sore Throats And Ear Problems*

---

# Synopsis

It is said that ear candling can relieve conditions affecting the ear, like earaches, tinnitus, excessive earwax, and glue ear. It is said to also benefit other conditions that affect the head area like colds, hay fever, headaches, sinus issues and snoring and is an extremely relaxing treatment in its own right. Physicians however say that there is no data to support this so let's look at the issue a bit further.

# Throat And Ears

Ear candling is said to open the ear canals and release pressure and help to carry off infection. Let's see how sore throat and ears are connected.

A sore throat or blocked ear is something which almost everybody has experienced at one time in life. A sore throat is an inflaming of the throat and most often it's painful. It's caused by viral or bacterial infections, fungal infection, or irritants like pollutants or chemical substance.

The throat is the common site for the infection to thrive when you're exposed to viruses or bacteria. You are able to get a sore throat if you come in contact with too much dust or any additional similar irritant.

If the raw throat is accompanied with a bad cold then your ears may get blocked. Antibiotics will help if it's a bacterial infection but they don't assist in case of viral infections.

In most cases, this trouble occurs as a reaction to a deeper fundamental problem. Therefore, it may likewise be said that a sore throat is really a symptom of underlying circumstances, like a bad cough, an upper respiratory infection, fever and pharyngitis too.

While a sore throat on its own is seldom serious, it may lead to a lot of discomfort, and trouble swallowing. This is likely what causes individuals to consult a doctor for help on how to eliminate a sore throat.

It's likewise quite common for individuals to suffer from a sore throat and ear issues at the same time.

Studies suggest that there's a direct relationship between sore throat and the ears, as the auditory tube, in the ear is connected directly to the ear. This tube executes the crucial function of keeping the fluid out of the middle ear.

Occasionally, a sore throat may cause this tube to swell up, which in turn leads to extra pressure, blockage and maybe even pain in the ear. Therefore, it's very common for individuals to suffer from both a sore throat and ear ache at the same time.

As a matter of fact the ears, nose as well as the throat are all closely associated and in case of any inflammation, infection or allergies affect one area; it's rather likely for all the parts to get impacted too.

For instance, the sinuses cavities or pockets, which are placed near the nose, are likewise connected to the ear and throat. Consequently, in case of a sinus infection, individuals all suffer from sore throat and blocked ears or clogged ears.

This is as the connection between all the 3 body parts allows the exchange of fluid between the 3 parts. This may likewise be the reason that a blocked nose may subsequently lead to a sore throat and ear issues.

Although a sore throat and ear trouble isn't very severe, it may lead to a lot of discomfort. Furthermore, a stuffy ear may likewise affect the ability to hear right. This may likewise cause an individual to call or visit a doctor, asking "my ear is clogged what should I do?" or "how do I unblock my ear". Some people advocate ear candling for this.

# Chapter 5:

*Ear Candling And Spirituality*

---

# Synopsis

Ear candling has been traced to the ancient Phoenicians, Egyptians and Chinese. Wall paintings, pottery and temple walls have depicted an individual sitting with an implement in the ear, with a flame on the end.  The Egyptians utilized ear candling for reaching the spirit world.

The priests and royalty were the only ones who were permitted to make contact with the spirit world consequently they were the only ones who'd have an ear candling done. While it is not recognized if they utilized ear candling for healing purposes, we do recognize it was utilized for spiritual purposes.

## The Spiritual Side

In North America we recognize from songs and stories that the Native Americans utilized ear candling as well. Not only was ear candling utilized for spiritual work and vision quests, they likewise utilized it for healing purposes.

In the Northwest the Native People utilize a clay cone and they place herbs inside which they burn and causes the smoke to coil down into the ear and withdraw the extra earwax and yeast from the body and or cause the vision quest to start.

In Mexico they utilize rolled up old paper to make their cones and they likewise place herbs inside and light it on fire to let it do its work.

Nowadays, in Germany, when a doctor is going through his internship part of his grooming is ear candling.

In England part of a nurses training is in how to execute an ear candling.

In the USA ear candling is a home remedy passed down from generation to generation and is executed mostly by lay individuals.

There are a lot of spiritual reasons for doing ear candling. Spiritual seekers and workers utilize ear candling to enhance E.S.P., second sight and others, as well as channeling and psychic powers.  As in the hands and feet, the ear bears nerve endings representative of all additional areas of the body.
Ear candling cleans away debris amassed on those nerve endings, thus clearing the way for currents of subtle energy to flow, unimpaired, to the body, brain and emotions.  Ear candling may heighten visualization and may balance and beef up the Chakras (energy centers) of the body.

# Chapter 6:



# Synopsis

Auriculotherapy or ear candling, likewise called ear coning is a folk medicine practice designated to reduce the "toxins" from within an individuals ear by means of a hollow candle placed in the ear.

It calls for placing one end of a hollow candle in the outer ear canal and lighting the other end. Ear candling is believed to be effective at producing a minor vacuum and getting rid of impurities from the ear.

A few critics claim their utilization has resulted in injuries, which naturally may be said about the use of just about any home cures that are utilized beyond the application of good sense.

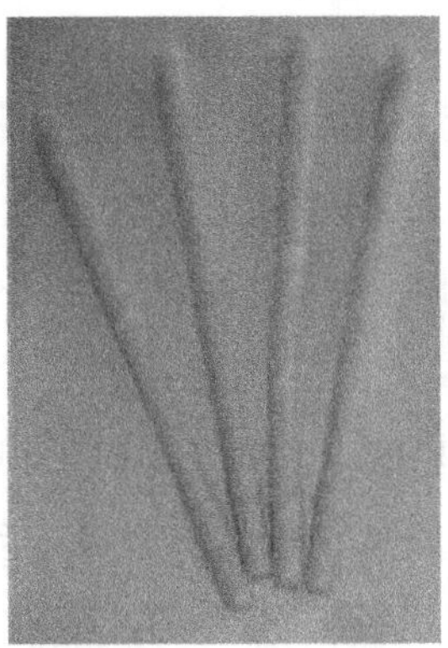

## How To And A Few Cautions

One end of a cylinder or cone of waxed cloth is put into the subject's ear, and the other end lit up. Commonly the subject is lying on one side with the treated ear upmost and the candle vertical, maybe stuck through a paper plate or aluminum pie tin to protect against hot wax or ash falling down the side.

A common ear candling session may last up to forty-five minutes, during which time a series of 1 or 2 ear candles might be burned for each ear. The experience has been reported as being kind of exotic, but pleasant and relaxing. One might hear some crackling and popping, or feel a little heat during the session.

**Caution**: Ear Candling shouldn't be done to individuals with medical ear tubes, perforated ear drums, or artificial ear drums.

Critics charge that the claims for ear candling are vague and even conflicting, and that no scientific studies have been done to document the health advantages.

Advocates claim significant betterment in their hearing, inner ear pain alleviation and a reduction in tinnitus symptoms after many ear candling sessions. It's curious why many studies haven't been conducted to evaluate the procedure scientifically, as it has been used for hundreds of years. It's suspected by several that some ear candle critics represent special vested interests with perceptible financial motives.

Ear candles are a home health care curative. Utilize common sense. Read all instructions and words of advice herein. If you don't feel comfortable - don't utilize them. If you don't feel secure in using fire around yourself and other people - don't utilize ear candles. If you don't know how to utilize ear candles - get help from somebody who does.

## Do's and Don'ts

- Never utilize them without a second individual who's able to supervise and/or help you.

- Utilize all cautions that an open fire calls for while utilizing an open flame.

- You'll need a glass of water, paper plate, and matches.

- Cut a cross in the middle of the paper plate large enough to put a candle in it snugly.

- The little end is pressed through the cut in the middle of the plate, and jutting through far enough to be put gently into the outer canal of the ear.

- Lie on your side, push all the hair away from the ear, light the ear taper and place the small end in the ear and hold gently between your fingers.

- Make sure you don't squeeze the candle.

- Make certain the little end is well seated in the ear making a great seal.

- Slant the cone somewhat, without breaching the seal.

- If you would like to massage the individual, massage along the forehead, brow, cheek bone, jaw bone, the side of the neck and the back of the neck constantly towards the ear. Don't move the head around. This ought to be a gentle and relaxing experience.

- Be heedful to the individual that's being candled.

- Once it burns down 7" take the taper out of the ear and snuff out the flame in a cup of water or a wet cloth.

- Cleanse the outside of the ear with your Q-tip, and if you like, place a few drops of Mullein, Garlic or Olive Oil in the ear.

- Don't place the Q-tip into the ear.

**<u>Don't use ear candles under any of the accompanying conditions.</u>**

- Cysts in the Ear
- Perforated Ear Drums
- Tumor of the Ear
- You're currently under the supervision of a MD for ear issues
- You're allergic to bee stings or honey.

# Chapter 7:

*What The Doctors Say*

---

# Synopsis

Ear candling, a method of treating upper respiratory issues is making a comeback. But a few physicians warn it might be unsafe.

## The Medical View

A lot of physicians state more research is required. The Food and Drug Administration states the practice isn't safe and considers the ear candle an unregulated medical device.

We're more concerned that the consumer be cognizant of what they're purchasing and that they be alerted to the fact that we trust these to be a substantial health risk, said an FDA physician.

The agency has adopted steps to forbid the sale and distribution of ear candles in the U.S.

Candles have been said to be linked to infections and punctured eardrums.

An Ear, nose and throat specialist got interested after seeing a lot of patients with traumas from ear candling.

The specific injuries seen were infection of the outside ear canal following utilization of these candles as well as a burn of the auditory canal. Physicians say that they have seen patients with holes in their eardrums after utilization of the candles.

One particular study was done to determine if an ear candle may in reality create a vacuum as practitioners claim.

The discovery of this particular study was that there was no vacuum, or negative pressure, rendered by a burning ear candle. It was likewise explored whether an ear candle in reality may draw out material from within the ear.

What was discovered was that no wax was moved out from their ear canal, and as a matter of fact some of the wax was pushed in deeper because of the placement of the ear candle.

Devotees swear it works however.

However even practicianers recommend caution. You have to make certain that you have an alternative practitioner or somebody who utilizes only the highest grade candles to do this practice.

However physicians have a different suggestion.

Their recommendation is that ear candles might be a nice thing to have on the dining room table while you are having dinner. They shouldn't be placed in the ear and decidedly shouldn't be utilized to try to cleanse the ear at all.

# Chapter 8:

## *Other Natural Ways Of Cleaning The Ear*

# Synopsis

There's an old saying that advises putting nothing in your ears littler than your elbow. Put differently, no one ought to use anything mechanical to remove ear wax or any other blockage from the deepest part of the ear canal.

Even the manufacturers of cotton swabs accent the danger of utilizing their products to get rid of ear wax deposits. There are times when one has to remove ear wax safely, all the same, particularly when it affects one's hearing or might lead to an infection.

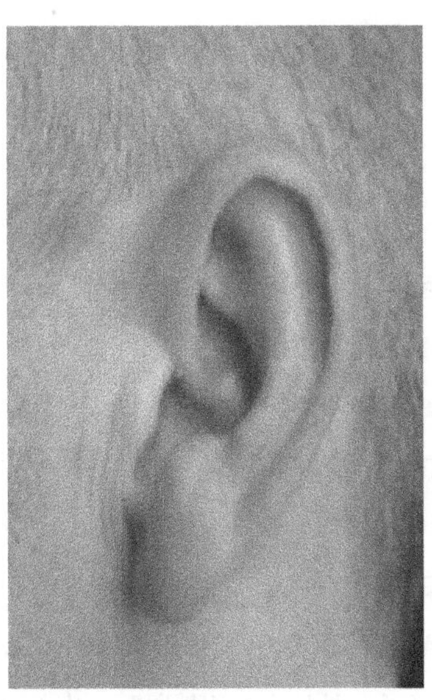

## Natural Ways

To remove ear wax safely, a few suggest utilizing warmed oils like baby oil, mineral oil or olive oil to weaken the ear wax. A couple of drops of warmed, however not hot; oil ought to be placed cautiously in the ear canal as the patient lies on his or her side.

The oil ought to be allowed to remain in the ear canal for a couple of seconds to literally dissolve the ear wax. To remove ear wax following the oil being applied, the patient ought to lean his or head to one side and let the oil flow out by nature into a clean cloth. A provision of clean water may then be squirted into the ear to remove ear wax deposits that might persist.

A different way to remove ear wax safely is to utilize ear drops specifically developed to soften excessive wax. These ear drops are commonly sold in the pharmacy section of a department or grocery, along with other ear care products for swimmer's ear and common earaches.

Implement these ear drops according to the directions on the box. As a whole, a solution is dropped into the ear canal to weaken and liquefy extra ear wax. After a couple of moments, the solution is allowed to run out of the ear naturally. A few products that take out ear wax might include a rubberized bulb for flushing out residue.

A few experts advise that the safest way to remove ear wax isn't to remove it at all. The body makes ear wax for a reason - to trap exterior dirt and additional contaminants before they may reach the tender workings of the inner ear. While a few might find this waxy substance unlikable, it is not always judicious to remove ear wax strictly for aesthetics. Utilizing a cotton swab to get rid of ear wax in the ear canal may lead to compression of the wax or puncture of the ear drum.

Conventional thought today is to remove ear wax only if it becomes unreasonable or compromises hearing. Discolored or unreasonable ear wax might be a sign of a bigger issue, so you might need to plan a visit to your personal doctor for a more thorough exam.

In the meantime, avoid utilizing anything mechanical to get rid of ear wax, like a paper clip, cotton swab or car key. A deep itch in the ear canal may frequently be alleviated by plugging your nose and blowing air through the Eustachian tubes. Unreasonable ear wax buildup may become a severe issue, so seek medical attention if these home remedies don't bring relief.

## Other Ways To Get Rid Of Stuffy Ears Naturally

Put a heating pad just below the affected ear, making a point that the heat isn't too high. The pad ought to only be placed on the area for about half-hour. The heat from the pad permeates the inner side of the ear canal, loosing the congestion that has led to a blocked ear. Rinsing with warm water, to which half a teaspoon of salt has been added, might also be effective.

# Wrapping Up

There are many views on the use of ear candling. Some swear by it, others swear by the fact that it should not be used. This has to be a personal decision. One should do a lot of good research where this issue is concerned and speak to a doctor prior to using any sort of treatment.

Do your homework and be safe with your precious hearing.

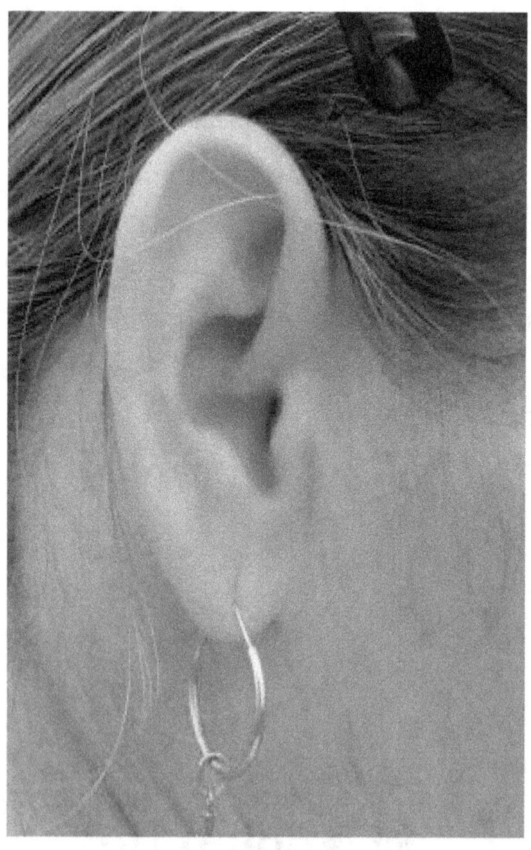